THE GOVERNMENT AND ITS PEOPLE
STUDY GUIDE

Mary Salamon

The Government and Its People
Study Guide
by Mary Salamon
Copyright © 2018 by Mary Salamon

ISBN-13: 9781727546873

Cover by Amani Hansen
Editing and layout by Jim Bryson

Volume I

How The Church Can Participate In Government

Chapter 1 – Worldviews

1.   Write out James Sire's quote on worldview, then rewrite it in your own words. What is your opinion on the definition of worldview?

2.   Do you believe that God controls everything? How does your belief affect your attitude toward government and government officials?

3.   What was the first governing institution created by God? In this institution, what was God's mandate?

4.   List some ways government is protective of a person's rights.

5.   What worldview do you have: "Come out and be Separate" or "Occupy till I come"? Explain your answer with examples in scripture.

Chapter 2 – Where Government Begins

In this chapter, the author states: "Whether we acknowledge it or not, rules and authority, seen and unseen, govern our lives every day. Everywhere a person walks, authority rules over him or her."

1. Do you agree with that statement? Why or why not?

2. Where do you acknowledge authority in your life?

3. List some rules that you have to observe in your life.

4. Do you believe the rules you listed are beneficial to the well-being of society? If not, explain why.

5. Colossians 1:16 : *"For by him all things were created, in heaven and on earth, visible and invisible, whether thrones or dominions or rulers or authorities—all things were created through him and for him."*

    The author gives definitions of all positions and places of authority in the world. Do a word study to find how these different positions and powers operate in the world today.

6. The author writes, "God, who is supreme and is all authority and has all authority, transferred authority to humankind to rule and govern by the order He set in motion when He created the earth. In all practicality, how do we as humans carry out our God-given dominion and authority? It is through the institution of government."

7.Do you agree or disagree with the premise that the Church has been given authority to rule and govern? Why or why not?

Chapter 3 Process

In this chapter the author delves deeply into process. "By definition, the word process means, 'continuous series of actions meant to accomplish some result.'"

1. This chapter discusses the micro and the macro of process in a person's life. Do you see how this works in your own personal life?

2. Describe your *micro* process.

3. Describe your macro process.

4. "A process exists for everything in this life. Nothing is seen that is without it. To deny process in our lives is to deny our existence."

   Do you agree with this statement? Why or why not?

Chapter 4- Joseph

1. According to the author, "The call and purpose of Joseph's life did not begin with Joseph." Where did it begin? Do you agree with the author's premise? Why or why not?

2. Joseph is given two dreams before he is taken into Egypt. The first dream offends his brothers and the second dream offends his father. Why were they offended?

3. Did both dreams come true in Joseph's life? Explain how.

4. When Joseph entered Potiphar's household he becomes an Asiatic slave. He probably was given the title of household servant. List the variety of tasks he would have been assigned.

5. Potiphar elevates Joseph to become the Steward over his entire household. This included two subsidiary titles. What were these titles?

6. What two primary things about Joseph indicate he was capable of filling these titles?

7. How does Joseph end up in prison?

8. Joseph finds favor with the keeper of the prison. The keeper elevates Joseph to the position of scribe of the prison. What duties did that position entail for Joseph?

9. Joseph was given the gifts of dreams and interpretation of dreams. Our God is amazing. Do you see the special positioning of Joseph being sent to prison unjustly?

10. Most people would not think that prison was a divine appointment from God. How does Joseph's prison sentence refute that belief?

11. After studying how each place in Egypt prepared Joseph for ruling in Egypt, how do you now view Joseph's process both in the micro and the macro?

Chapter 5 - Moses

1. In the first paragraph of this chapter, the author lists various offices or roles Moses occupied. List these offices.

2. How did Moses become a prince in Egypt?

3. Moses's training was extensive in Egypt. His education came from the officials of the land. List the instruction and type of education he received.

4. In modern times, what kind of degrees or vocations did Moses qualify for?

5. According to Westbrook and Wells in their book "Everyday Law," seven law codes have been recovered. List the seven codes.

6. In the Laws of Hammurabi from the city of Babylon, one law that states, "If a man destroys the eye of another man, they shall destroy his eye." This is the same law as the law from Moses that states, "eye for eye, tooth for tooth." Some say that Moses just copied the law, while others say that Moses wasn't even aware of the writing of the law. Which is your opinion? Why?

7. After reading this chapter on Moses, how has your perspective changed about his role as a legislator and lawgiver?

Chapter 6 - Deborah

1. The scripture states in Judges 3 that the Lord left foreign nations to test Israel so they would learn the art of war. Do you believe there is a spiritual counterpart to Christians today? Give some examples.

2. Describe the cycle from beginning to end that the people of Israel found themselves in as described in the book of Judges.

3. Although the deliverers and heroes were titled judges, none of them presided in the office of judge except for one, Deborah. Deborah, like Moses, had other roles. List the roles that Deborah functioned in other than a judge.

4. Deborah's name means "bee," and the Scripture says that she was the "wife of Lapidot." The Hebrew words are *eset lapidot,* which could also mean "woman of torches." Given Deborah's role in history the author believes the term means "fiery woman." There is quite a difference between "wife of Lapidot" and "woman of torches." Which definition of Deborah do you prefer?

5. Depending on the definition you chose, how does your view of Deborah differ from what your view might be under the other definition?

6. Is it possible Deborah was a fiery woman married to a man named Lapidot?

7. "Deborah rose as 'a mother in Israel.' Another Scripture that coincides with the term 'mother in Israel,' is 2 Samuel 20:18-19. Read the Scripture, and explain the similarities of what it meant to be a "mother in Israel," whether it is a person or a place.

8. Deborah's judicial role was compared to that of a mother. How differently do people perceive receiving judgment from a mother figure versus a father figure?

9. According to Isaiah 1, what did the judges do that displeased the Lord?

10. Do you think that some judges today displease the Lord? If yes, give examples of how modern judges can displease or even grieve the Lord.

Chapter 7 - David and Solomon

1. In Acts 13:22, Paul explains that David was specifically handpicked by the Lord. Why?

2. Besides becoming the natural king to the nation of Israel, what other things were promised to David?

3. How far and wide in scope is the promise to David by God?

4. In Luke 19:11-27, those that occupy till the Lord's return and are faithful receive rewards. What are the rewards?

5. If the reward is more responsibility in rulership, what does that speak to you about the kind of people the Lord is training and setting apart for Himself for all eternity?

6. What is the consequence to the one who hid his talent?

7. Why do you think the Lord seems severe with the person that hid his talent?

8. What is the basic definition of justice?

9. In this chapter, what is the definition of injustice?

10. Do you agree with this definition? Why or why not?

11. Define the three types of justice. How do they differ from one another?

12. The tenth commandment is about covetousness. Do you think this could be the root of most of the injustice in the world? Explain why or why not.

Chapter 8 - Elijah

Elijah was not a king or official in Israel's government. He was chosen by God to be a national prophet and hero. He was given governmental authority to judge two of the most powerful kings and queens of his time.

Every act of Elijah was ordained to confront and challenge deeply held beliefs concerning Baal. He challenged the people by stating openly that they were vacillating between two beliefs, and he was ordained by God to show openly that there was no Baal to cry to, that he existed only in their minds.

1. List some of the acts of Elijah that displayed the power of God and confirmed Elijah's authority.

2. Today Christians have authority and rights. Christians have spiritual rights, and Americans have Yes, natural rights. The Bill of Rights lists the rights of American citizens. The very first amendment is about religious freedom. Find a copy of the Bill of Rights, and discuss the difference between your rights as a believer and your rights as an American citizen.

3. When called upon, Elijah obeyed God and confronted the highest governmental authority in the nation of Israel. Do you see any resemblance to this kind of confrontation in our nation today?

Chapter 9 - Daniel

"Daniel and his companions were brought into the highest level of Babylonian government. Their names were changed, and they were expected to serve and obey the king and his rule of law, learn the culture of Babylon, and live in and with that culture." The Chaldean culture included magicians, sorcerers, and enchanters. They used omens, incantations, and other occult practices including astrology to tell the future and search for hidden mysteries in the dark.

Daniel was light brought into the midst of darkness. It was impossible for him to "Come out from among them and be separate."

1. What does this show about the grace of God on a servant's life?

2. Daniel and his companions refused to eat at the king's table. This was not a small slight. It could have cost the life of the official in charge. Why did Daniel and his companions take such a risk?

3. Daniel served as an advisor to four kings. What does that tell you about the character and integrity of Daniel?

4. List the four kings he served.

5. Which king do you think Daniel impacted the most by his faith in God? Why?

6. Daniel is known as a major prophet. He was a deep visionary. His was chosen to prophesy world events and the coming of the Lord. He spent hours in prayer. He was known throughout the Persian Empire as a man full of wisdom and knowledge. He did all this while serving in a secular government. How does this speak to men and women who desire to be in full-time ministry and think they have to be in a pulpit to do it?

7. Faith is an act. List the key words the author highlights to display the actions which correspond with the faith that Daniel and his companions displayed.

Chapter 10 - Esther

1. What is different about the book of Esther that commentators have noticed?

2. How do we know that Esther and Mordecai had no desire to leave Susa?

3. What did it mean for Mordecai to sit at the gate of the palace?

4. What do gates represent in the Bible?

5. List some of the inconsistencies in the book of Ester regarding the things Christians know are direct disobedience to God.

6. When studying the book of Esther, one sees definite gray areas. Does this change your view on how the Lord positions people? Or did Mordecai and Esther position themselves?

7. What example does the author use when comparing how Mordecai brought Esther in before the king?

8. Is it fair to judge Esther and Mordecai in light of other Scripture in the Bible? Why or why not?

9. In the book of Esther, role reversals happen. What two prominent positions were completely reversed?

10. Haman and Mordecai are bitter enemies. There is history between them. Explain this history.

11. Esther became the wife of King Ahasuerus. She influenced the king in three distinct, powerful ways. Describe all three and how one of them is important to the Jewish people to this day.

Chapter 11 - Nehemiah

Nehemiah was the cupbearer of Artaxerxes I.

1. Describe the duties of a cupbearer.

2. In Nehemiah 1, Nehemiah was given a report on the condition of Jerusalem. The walls were broken down and the gates were burned with fire. What was the first thing Nehemiah did when he heard the report?

3. When Nehemiah went before the king to make requests on behalf of his people, he received everything he asked for. The author describes specific keys on why Nehemiah received favor from the king. Describe the keys.

4. What were the different types of people and groups Nehemiah brought together to rebuild the wall?

5. Do you believe this is a gift of great leadership?

6. Name some strengths Nehemiah would have had to display to bring such a diverse group together.

7. How did Nehemiah deal with the opposition from without?

8. How did Nehemiah deal with the opposition from within?

9. How was Nehemiah a noble example as the governor of Judah?

10. According to the author, what Nehemiah accomplished is a miracle of God. Do you agree? Why or why not?

11. Nehemiah completed the wall in fifty-two days. List the other accomplishments he achieved while in Jerusalem.

Chapter 12 - Apostle Paul and Romans 13

1. At the time Romans 13 was written by the Apostle Paul, who was in charge of Rome?

2. Read Romans 13:1-7. Do you believe it is about quiet submission to civil pagan leaders? Explain your reasoning.

3. What do some theologians believe about the way Paul addresses the beginning of Romans?

4. Roman 13:1 states that no authority exists that hasn't been instituted by God. Is every person that carries civil authority a servant of God? If not, why?

5. Paul exhorts the Church to participate fully in Rome as citizens. We know this by the things he asked the Church to do. In verse 7 of Romans 13, what are things he commands the Church that shows a high level of engagement in Roman society?

6. Do you believe Christians today should do the same things that the Roman believers were exhorted to do?

7. At what point should Christians disobey civil authority?

Volume II

How The Church Can
Participate In Government

46

The Government and Its People – Study Guide

Introduction to Volume II

1. The author discusses the fact that soil will grow weeds if purposeful and intentional planting is not done. If soil is symbolic of our everyday life, family and heart, what will spring up as weeds if these symbolic gardens are not tended?

2. Give an example that you have witnessed when a person in authority goes AWOL and doesn't take responsibility for their position or power.

3. In your experience and opinion; what does it mean to be present?

4. The author lists four distinct things salt was and is used for. Symbolically Christians are called to be the "salt of the earth". List several ways how that would look in everyday life.

5. Romans 13 discusses the role of civil authority. Do you agree that civil servants are God's servants? Why or why not?

6. Romans 13:1 *The authorities that exist have been established by God.* List some positions and duties that you think are established by God in Civil Government.

7. Are civil servants on the same playing field as ministry servants? Be specific in why they are or are not.

Chapter 13- Prayer

1. In December 1944, General Patton called upon his officer, Paul D. Hawkins, to pray. What was the prayer request and how was it answered?

2. The author lists five things comparing war to the game of chess. List those five things.

    1-

    2-

    3-

    4-

    5-

3. How does the author compare a pawn on a chess board to prayer?

4. What does 1 Timothy 2:2 promise if we pray for kings and those in authority?

5. Do you think the future is fixed or free? Explain your answer in detail?

6. The author believes that the future is not fixed. There are six scriptures listed that describe cause and effect. Pick three and write out the cause and effect of each statement.

7. The author believes that a Christians can change God's mind. Do you agree or disagree? Why?

8. The author lists three people in scripture who changed God's mind. What were the things they pleaded with the Lord to not do?

9. If the future is fixed, why did Daniel have to pray and fast for the return of God's people to their homeland? What events took place in the heavenly realm when Daniel prayed?

10. Why is specific prayer important?

Chapter 14 - Vote

1. "The vote is the most powerful instrument ever devised by man for breaking down injustice." Lyndon Baines Johnson Do you agree or disagree with this the quote? What types of injustice are broken down through the vote?

2. In 1840, there were three specific things women were not allowed to do in civil government. List those three things.

3. What did the Thirteenth and Fourteenth Amendments achieve?

4. What did the Fifteenth Amendment achieve and what rift did it cause within women's suffrage movement at that time?

5. What two industries were against women voting and why?

6. How did the media depict women of the suffrage movement? What did some say of the husbands that supported their wives?

7. How many years was the Susan B. Anthony Amendment brought up before Congress?

8. The fight for the woman vote in Tennessee became known as the "War of the Roses." Describe in detail what that meant.

9. What was the name of the congressman that cast the deciding vote? What was his reason for his decision?

10. It is a known fact that many women in the suffrage movement were strong Christians. They came out of the church pew and started a political firestorm. Do you believe God was leading them? What other political movements have the thumbprints of God on them?

11. The author lists four reasons why a person doesn't vote. List those reasons and some attitudes people have for not voting.

12. The author lists nine things where the vote is counted. List those nine things and write a short essay about one of the things you have seen changed in your life from the vote.

Chapter 15 – Citizen Lobbyist

1. A law was passed in New York state in 1997 which involved a tabby cat named Buster. What law was passed because of what happened to Buster?

2. What is the definition of a "citizen lobbyist"?

3. The author lists two laws that are named after someone. Who are they? What happened to them and what laws were instituted?

4. What drives people to become lobbyists?

5. What is the first step in advocating for an issue?

6. The author lists several questions when advocating for an issue. List those questions.

7. What is a petition and what four things do you need to understand before doing a petition?

8. Another way to get involved is by joining a non-profit organization that has similar values as your own. What are some of the things that organizations offer Citizen Lobbyists?

9. Social media is a powerful tool for Citizen Lobbyists. List some of the guidelines when using a social media platform.

10. There are three types of legislators, describe all three.

11. What are the four distinct ways to educate a legislator?

12. What five things will the undecided legislator consider before casting a vote?

13. What are the three ways to reach out to legislators?

Chapter 16 - The Neighborhood

1. This chapter opens up with a powerful story of a neighbor saving a child's life. Do you have similar stories with your neighbors?

2. Why do you think neighbors don't get to know each other?

3. Has social media changed the local neighborhood? If so, in what ways?

4. What is the definition of neighbor in the parable of the "Good Samaritan"?

5. There are several ideas listed to start the salvation process with neighbors. What are some you would like to do?

Chapter 17 - City Government

1. Mayors are leaders of the city and are to be community and political leaders. Describe the four roles of a Mayor. After studying the roles of office of the mayor has your opinion changed about what they do?

2. The City Council is what branch of government?

3. List three things a city council does and study them fully for your city. How does their authority affect your everyday life?

4. Policeman do more than just drive around in cars and drink coffee with donuts. List three things police do that are important to the community.

5. Pick a department discussed in this chapter and compare the similarities and differences to the department in your city.

6. How does the Lord watch over the city?

Chapter 18 - The Schools

1. Christian students in public schools have been challenged due to their faith in different instances. What are some of the challenges of the cases that have been brought to court?

2. In this chapter there is a quote: "Students do not shed their constitutional rights to freedom of speech or expression at the schoolhouse gate." Do you agree or disagree? Why?

3. Who is the highest authority over children?

4. The author describes a defensive tactic in raising children and an offensive tactic. Describe both tactics?

5. What are some of the things a school board is responsible for? Why is it important to become a school board member?

6. What does the PTA stand for? What does the PTA do? Why would it be a great idea for parents to participate in the PTA?

7. What is the value of participating in organized sports for children? How can parents get actively involved in their children's extra-curriculum events?

Chapter 19 - State and National Government

1. Name the three Branches of the United States Government.

2. What other things come in groups of three that the author didn't write?

3. In the author's opinion, the most significant way the number three is shown is with Jesus Christ the Lord; crucified, buried and rose on the third day. Do you agree or disagree? Why?

4. Where did the original idea come for the three branches of government? There are two sources- list them.

5. The author believes that the three Branch of Government are found in scripture. Write out that scripture and compare it to our three Branch of Government today.

6. Write an essay how the Godhead is ruling as King, Judge and Lawgiver in various ways through the scripture. (Note: Use pages at end of book.)

7. What are the names of the three that rule the entire universes.

8. List the positions in the Executive Branch in the United States Government.

9. List the positions in the Legislative Branch in the United States Government.

10. List the positions in the Judicial Branch in the United States Government.

11. What is the title of a person who is elected head of a singular state?

12. If a person aspires to lead at the State or Federal level, he or she must start at the community level. List two things a person can do in their community to start their participation in the political process.

13. What is a PCO and what do they do?

14. Why is education important to hold a political post?

15. What is an intern in government? What are some of the things they do?

16. List some things families can do to learn about the importance of participating in government.

Chapter 20 - International Government

1. The author mentions three places in the world where Christians are being persecuted for their faith. List those three places?

2. John Christopher Stevens served only 3 ½ months in Benghazi before he was killed. List his experience, education and background.

3. List three things a diplomat does.

4. List three things an ambassador does.

5. We are ambassadors for Christ. Write a short essay on what that would look like in the role of a US ambassador.

Made in the USA
Columbia, SC
26 May 2022

60881475R00046